RECIPES FROM
GRANDMA'S KITCHEN
A SAMPLER OF TIMELESS AMERICAN HOME COOKING

RECIPES FROM
GRANDMA'S KITCHEN
A Sampler of Timeless American Home Cooking

CONSULTANT EDITOR: LINDLEY BOEGEHOLD

SMITHMARK

This edition published in 1995 by
SMITHMARK Publishers Inc.
16 East 32nd Street
New York, NY 10016

SMITHMARK books are available for bulk purchase for sales promotion and for premium use.
For details write or call the Manager of Special Sales, SMITHMARK Publishers Inc., 16 East 32nd Street,
New York, NY, 10016; (212) 532-6600.

ISBN 0 8317 7458 4

Publisher: Joanna Lorenz
Editorial Manager: Helen Sudell
Designer: Nigel Partridge
Photographer: Amanda Haywood and David F. Wisse, Picture Perfect, USA (p 6/7)
Illustrations by: Estelle Corke
Recipes by: Carla Capalbo and Laura Washburn

Printed and bound in Singapore

Contents

—

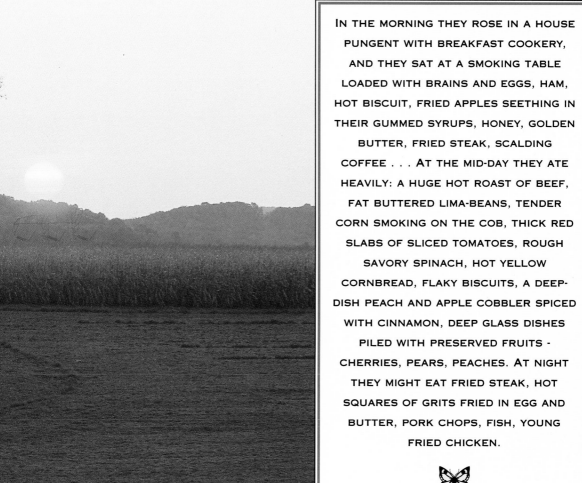

IN THE MORNING THEY ROSE IN A HOUSE
PUNGENT WITH BREAKFAST COOKERY,
AND THEY SAT AT A SMOKING TABLE
LOADED WITH BRAINS AND EGGS, HAM,
HOT BISCUIT, FRIED APPLES SEETHING IN
THEIR GUMMED SYRUPS, HONEY, GOLDEN
BUTTER, FRIED STEAK, SCALDING
COFFEE . . . AT THE MID-DAY THEY ATE
HEAVILY: A HUGE HOT ROAST OF BEEF,
FAT BUTTERED LIMA-BEANS, TENDER
CORN SMOKING ON THE COB, THICK RED
SLABS OF SLICED TOMATOES, ROUGH
SAVORY SPINACH, HOT YELLOW
CORNBREAD, FLAKY BISCUITS, A DEEP-
DISH PEACH AND APPLE COBBLER SPICED
WITH CINNAMON, DEEP GLASS DISHES
PILED WITH PRESERVED FRUITS -
CHERRIES, PEARS, PEACHES. AT NIGHT
THEY MIGHT EAT FRIED STEAK, HOT
SQUARES OF GRITS FRIED IN EGG AND
BUTTER, PORK CHOPS, FISH, YOUNG
FRIED CHICKEN.

FROM *LOOK HOMEWARD, ANGEL*
BY THOMAS WOLFE, 1929

SPLIT PEA SOUP

—

THIS HEARTY SOUP MAKES A MEAL IN ITSELF. SERVE WITH PARMESAN TOASTS AND A MUG OF HOT CIDER.

SERVES 8

1 pound dried green split peas

2 quarts water

1 ham bone with some meat left on it, or 1 ham hock

1 cup minced onion

1 cup sliced leeks

½ cup finely sliced celery

¼ cup fresh parsley sprigs

1 teaspoon salt

6 black peppercorns

2 bay leaves

Rinse the split peas under cold running water. Discard any discolored peas. Place the peas in a large kettle and add water to cover. Bring to a boil and boil 2 minutes. Remove from the heat and let soak 1 hour. Drain.

Put the peas back in the kettle and add the measured water, ham bone or hock, onion, leeks, celery, parsley, salt, peppercorns, and bay leaves (see below left). Bring to a boil. Reduce the heat, cover, and simmer gently until the peas are tender, about 1-1½ hours. Skim occasionally.

Remove the bay leaves and the ham bone or hock from the soup. Cut the meat off the bone, discarding any fat, and chop the meat into fine pieces. Set aside. Discard the ham bone and the bay leaves.

Purée the soup in batches in a food processor or blender. Pour into a clean saucepan and add the chopped ham. Check the seasoning, adding more salt and pepper as required. Simmer the soup 3-4 minutes to heat through before serving.

CLASSIC CHICKEN NOODLE SOUP

—

THIS IS THE PERFECT DISH FOR ANYTHING THAT AILS YOU, A COLD, A SORE THROAT, OR EVEN A
DRAB GREY MOOD. A STEAMING FRAGRANT BOWL SOMEHOW MAKES EVERYTHING A LITTLE BETTER.

10

SERVES 8

1 3-pound chicken, cut in pieces

2 onions, quartered

1 parsnip, quartered

2 carrots, quartered

½ teaspoon salt

1 bay leaf

2 allspice berries

4 black peppercorns

3 quarts water

1 cup very thin egg noodles

sprigs of fresh dill, for garnishing

In a large stockpot, combine the chicken pieces, onions, parsnip, carrots, salt, bay leaf, allspice berries and peppercorns.

Add the water to the pot and bring to a boil, skimming frequently.

Reduce the heat to low and simmer 1½ hours, skimming occasionally.

Strain the broth through a fine-mesh strainer into a bowl. Refrigerate overnight.

When the chicken pieces are cool enough to handle, cut away the meat from the bones. Discard all of the bones, skin, vegetables, and flavorings.

Chop the chicken meat and refrigerate overnight. Remove the solidified fat from the surface of the chilled broth. Pour the broth into a saucepan and bring to a boil. Taste the broth; if a more concentrated flavor is wanted, boil 10 minutes to reduce slightly.

Add the chicken meat and noodles to the broth (see above) and cook until the noodles are tender, about 8 minutes (check individual package directions for timing). Serve hot, garnished with dill sprigs.

ROAST PORK AND COLESLAW SANDWICHES

—

LEFTOVERS NEVER TASTED BETTER THAN THESE OVERSTUFFED SANDWICHES. SERVE WITH SOME
DILL PICKLES AND POTATO CHIPS.

12

SERVES 6

¾ cup mayonnaise

2 tablespoons catsup

¼-½ teaspoon cayenne

1 tablespoon light brown sugar

1 pound roast pork, thinly sliced

1 pound green or white cabbage, cut in wedges

2 carrots, finely shredded

1 small green bell pepper, seeded and diced

½ small red onion, finely chopped

12 small round Italian or French bread rolls,
    split open

In a large bowl, combine the mayonnaise, catsup, cayenne, and brown sugar. Stir together well.

Stack the slices of roast pork. With a sharp knife, cut them into matchstick strips.

Remove the cores from the cabbage wedges. Lay the wedges on a chopping board and cut into fine strips across the leaves.

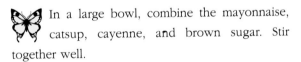

Add the pork, cabbage, carrots, green bell pepper, and red onion to the mayonnaise mixture. Toss to mix (see above).

Fill the split bread rolls with the pork coleslaw and serve immediately.

VARIATIONS

INSTEAD OF ROAST PORK SANDWICHES, TRY SUBSTITUTING SLICES OF COOKED HAM OR TURKEY, AND PREPARE THEM AS ABOVE. OR FOR A CHANGE OF PACE, TRY TUNA IN PLACE OF MEAT.

CLUB SANDWICHES

—

THESE CLASSIC TRIPLE-DECKERS CAN BE MODIFIED IN MANY WAYS. SOME SLICED AVOCADO, OR
SOME LEAVES OF RADICCHIO, OR MANGO CHUTNEY — LET YOUR IMAGINATION RUN RIOT.

14

SERVES 4

8 bacon slices

12 slices of white bread or rectangular brioche,
   toasted

½ cup mayonnaise

¼-½ pound cooked chicken breast meat, sliced

8 large lettuce leaves

salt and pepper

1 beefsteak tomato, cut across in 4 slices

 In a heavy skillet, fry the bacon until crisp
and the fat is rendered. Place the bacon on
paper towels to drain.

Lay 4 slices of toast on a flat surface. Spread them with some of
the mayonnaise.

Top each slice with one-quarter
of the chicken and a lettuce leaf.
Season with salt and pepper
to taste.

Spread 4 of the remaining
toast slices with mayonnaise.
Lay them on top of the lettuce.

Top each sandwich with a slice of tomato, 2
bacon slices, and another lettuce leaf (see left).

Spread the remaining slices of toast with the rest
of the mayonnaise. Place them on top of the sandwiches, mayonnaise-side down.

Cut each sandwich into four triangles and secure
each triangle with a toothpick.

COOK'S TIP

IF WATCHING CALORIES, TRY USING A LOW-CALORIE
MAYONNAISE - YOU WILL LOSE NONE OF THE FLAVOR.

CORNMEAL-COATED COD WITH TOMATO SAUCE

—

THIS IS A DELICIOUS AND HEALTHY WAY TO FRY FISH. THE LIGHTLY ACID TOMATO SAUCE
COMPLEMENTS THE CORNMEAL CRUST PERFECTLY.

16

SERVES 4

3 tablespoons cornmeal

½ teaspoon salt

¼ teaspoon hot chili powder or cayenne

4 cod steaks, each 1 inch thick (about 1½ pounds)

2 tablespoons corn oil

fresh basil sprigs, for garnishing

FOR THE TOMATO SAUCE

2 tablespoons olive oil

1 shallot or ½ small onion, finely chopped

1 garlic clove, minced

1 pound ripe tomatoes, chopped, or 1
*   16-ounce can crushed tomatoes*

⅛ teaspoon sugar

¼ cup dry white wine

2 tablespoons chopped fresh basil or ½ teaspoon
*   dried basil*

salt and pepper

For the sauce, heat the oil in a saucepan. Add the shallot or onion and the garlic and cook until soft, about 5 minutes. Stir in the tomatoes, sugar, wine, and basil. Bring to a boil. Simmer until thickened, 10-15 minutes.

Work the sauce through a vegetable mill or strainer until smooth. Return it to the pan. Season with salt and pepper. Set aside.

Combine the cornmeal, salt, and chili powder or cayenne on a sheet of wax paper.

Rinse the cod steaks, then dip them on both sides into the cornmeal mixture, patting gently to make an even coating.

Heat the corn oil in a large frying pan. Add the cod steaks and cook until golden brown and the flesh will flake easily when tested with a fork, about 5 minutes on each side. Cook in batches if necessary. Meanwhile, reheat the tomato sauce.

Garnish the cod steaks with basil sprigs and serve with the tomato sauce.

VARIATION

IN PLACE OF COD, USE MONKFISH, CUT INTO STEAKS OR
THICK FILLETS - IT TASTES JUST AS GOOD.

BAKED STUFFED TROUT

—

WHEN BUYING TROUT MAKE SURE THE EYES ARE CLEAR AND FULL AND THE SKIN IS SHINY.
IT MUST BE ABSOLUTELY FRESH AS ITS FLAVOR IS VERY DELICATE.

18

SERVES 4

2 tablespoons butter or margarine

1 onion, chopped

1 celery stick, diced

2 slices of fresh bread cubes

1 tablespoon fresh thyme leaves, or 1 teaspoon
dried thyme

salt and pepper

4 trout, dressed (about ½ pound each)

        8 bacon slices

        celery leaves or parsley, for
        garnishing

Preheat the oven to 450°F.
Melt the butter or margarine in a skillet.
Add the onion and celery and
cook until softened, about 5 minutes.
Remove the pan from the heat. Add the
bread cubes and thyme, and season with salt
and pepper to taste. Stir to mix well.

Thoroughly season the cavity of
each trout with salt and pepper.

Stuff each trout with the bread mixture, dividing
it evenly between the fish (see above). If necessary,
secure the openings with wooden toothpicks.
Wrap 2 bacon slices around each stuffed
trout. Arrange in a baking dish.
Bake until the fish flakes easily and
the bacon is crisp, 35-40 minutes.
Serve garnished with celery
leaves or sprigs of parsley.

BREADED FISH WITH TARTARE SAUCE —

COD IS THE TRADITIONAL FISH USED IN THIS TASTY RECIPE, BUT FLOUNDER OR HADDOCK FILLETS
ARE EXCELLENT AS WELL. SERVE WITH CREAMED SPINACH ON THE SIDE.

20

SERVES 4

½ cup dry bread crumbs

1 teaspoon dried oregano

½ teaspoon cayenne

1 cup milk

2 teaspoons salt

4 pieces of cod fillet (about 1½ pounds)

3 tablespoons butter or margarine, melted

FOR THE TARTARE SAUCE

½ cup mayonnaise

½ teaspoon Dijon-style mustard

1 kosher dill pickle spear, finely chopped

1 tablespoon drained capers, chopped

1 teaspoon chopped fresh parsley

1 teaspoon chopped fresh chives

1 teaspoon chopped fresh tarragon

salt and pepper

Preheat the oven to 450°F. Grease a shallow glass or porcelain baking dish.

Combine the bread crumbs, oregano, and cayenne on a plate and blend together. Mix the milk with the salt in a bowl, stirring well for a few minutes to dissolve the salt.

Dip the pieces of cod fillet in the milk, then transfer to the plate and coat with the bread crumb mixture (see below). Arrange the coated fish in the prepared baking dish, in one layer. Drizzle the melted butter or margarine evenly over the fish.

Bake until the fish flakes easily when tested with a fork, 10-15 minutes.

Meanwhile, for the tartare sauce, combine all the ingredients in a small bowl. Stir gently to mix well.

Serve the fish while still hot, accompanied by the tartare sauce.

CRAB CAKES

—

MAKE SURE YOU USE ABSOLUTELY FRESH CRAB MEAT FOR THIS QUINTESSENTIALLY
MARYLAND DISH.

22

SERVES 3 OR 6

1 pound fresh lump crab meat

1 egg, well beaten

1 teaspoon Dijon-style mustard

2 teaspoons prepared horseradish

2 teaspoons Worcestershire sauce

8 scallions, finely chopped

¼ cup chopped fresh parsley

1½ cups fresh bread crumbs

salt and pepper

1 tablespoon whipping cream (optional)

½ cup dry bread crumbs

3 tablespoons butter or margarine

lemon wedges, for serving

In a mixing bowl, combine the crab meat, egg, mustard, horseradish, Worcestershire sauce, scallions, parsley, fresh bread crumbs, and seasoning. Mix gently, leaving the pieces of crab meat as large as possible. If the mixture is too dry to hold together, add the cream.

Divide the crab mixture into 6 portions and shape into patties.

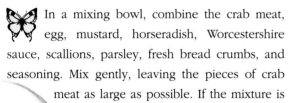

Put the dry bread crumbs on a plate. Coat the crab cakes on both sides with crumbs (see above).

Melt the butter or margarine in a skillet. Fry the crab cakes until golden, about 3 minutes on each side. Add more fat if necessary.

Serve 1 or 2 per person, with lemon wedges.

COOK'S TIP

FOR EASIER HANDLING AND TO MAKE THE CRAB MEAT
GO FURTHER, ADD AN EXTRA CUP OF FRESH BREAD-
CRUMBS AND 1 MORE EGG TO THE CRAB MIXTURE.

BAKED PORK LOIN WITH RED CABBAGE AND APPLES

THIS FRAGRANT WINTER DISH IS A GERMAN CLASSIC. THE RED CABBAGE ABSORBS THE PORK JUICES AND BECOMES TENDER AND SWEET.

SERVES 8

4½-pound boned loin of pork

½ teaspoon ground ginger

salt and pepper

4 tablespoons butter, melted

about 1½ cups sweet apple cider or dry white wine

FOR THE CABBAGE

3 tablespoons butter or margarine

1½ cups finely sliced onions

1 teaspoon caraway seeds

3 tart-sweet apples, quartered, cored, and sliced

1 tablespoon dark brown sugar

3½-pound head of red cabbage, cored and shredded

6 tablespoons cider vinegar, or ¼ cup wine vinegar and 2 tablespoons water

½ cup beef stock

½ cup sweet apple cider or dry white wine

1 teaspoon salt

¼ teaspoon fresh or dried thyme leaves

Preheat the oven to 350°F.

Trim any excess fat from the pork roast. Sprinkle with the ginger, salt, and pepper.

Place the pork, fat side down, in a large Dutch oven. Cook over medium heat, turning frequently, until browned on all sides, about 15 minutes. Add a little of the melted butter if the roast starts to stick.

Cover, transfer to the oven, and roast for 1 hour, basting frequently with the pan drippings, melted butter, and cider or wine.

Meanwhile, to prepare the cabbage, melt the butter or margarine in a large skillet and add the onions and caraway seeds. Cook over low heat until softened, 8-10 minutes. Stir in the apple slices and brown sugar. Cover the pan and cook 4-5 minutes more.

Stir in the cabbage. Add the vinegar. Cover and cook 10 minutes. Pour in the stock and cider or wine, add the salt and thyme leaves, and stir well. Cover again and cook over medium-low heat 30 minutes.

Remove the pot from the oven. Transfer the roast to a plate and keep hot. Tilt the pot and spoon off and discard all but 2 tablespoons of the fat.

Transfer the cabbage mixture from the skillet to the Dutch oven and stir well to mix thoroughly with the roasting juices.

Place the pork roast on top of the layer of cabbage. Cover and return to the oven. Cook another hour, basting occasionally with cider or wine.

PORK CHOPS WITH SAUERKRAUT

—

THE PUNGENCY OF THE SAUERKRAUT PERFECTLY SETS OFF THE PORK IN THIS VERY GERMAN PREPARATION. IT CALLS FOR A TALL GLASS OF COLD BEER, PREFERABLY A PILSENER.

26

SERVES 6

6 bacon slices, coarsely chopped

3 tablespoons flour

salt and pepper

6 boned top-loin pork chops or sirloin cutlets

2 teaspoons light brown sugar

1 garlic clove, minced

1½ pounds sauerkraut, rinsed

1 teaspoon juniper berries

1 teaspoon black peppercorns

1 cup beer

1 cup chicken stock

Preheat the oven to 350°F.

In a skillet, fry the bacon until just beginning to brown. With a slotted spoon, transfer the bacon to a casserole dish.

Season the flour with salt and pepper. Coat the pork chops with the seasoned flour, shaking off any excess. Brown the chops in the bacon fat, about 5 minutes on each side. Remove and drain on paper towels.

Add the brown sugar and garlic to the fat in the skillet and cook, stirring, for about 3 minutes. Add the sauerkraut, juniper berries, and peppercorns.

Transfer the sauerkraut mixture to the casserole and mix with the bacon. Lay the pork chops on top. Pour on top the beer and chicken stock (see left).

Place the casserole in the oven and cook until the chops are very tender, 45-55 minutes.

COOK'S TIP

SERVE WITH PLENTY OF FRESH GREEN VEGETABLES THAT HAVE BEEN LIGHTLY STEAMED.

BAKED SAUSAGES AND BEANS WITH CRISPY TOPPING

ALL THIS HEARTY CASSEROLE NEEDS FOR ACCOMPANIMENT IS A GREEN SALAD, AND PERHAPS A PIECE OF SHARP CHEDDAR CHEESE.

SERVES 6

2 cups dry navy beans or Great Northern beans, soaked overnight and drained

1 onion, stuck with 4 cloves

3 tablespoons butter or margarine

1 pound pork link sausages

1 pound kielbasa sausage, cut into ½-inch slices

¼ pound bacon, chopped

1 large onion, finely chopped

2 garlic cloves, minced

1 16-ounce can crushed tomatoes

½ cup tomato paste

¼ cup maple syrup

2 tablespoons dark brown sugar

½ teaspoon mustard powder

¼ teaspoon salt

pepper

½ cup fresh bread crumbs

Put the beans in a saucepan and cover with fresh cold water. Add the clove-studded onion. Bring the water to a boil and continue to boil until the beans are just tender, about 1 hour. Drain the beans and discard the onion.

Preheat the oven to 350°F.

Melt half of the butter or margarine in a large flameproof casserole. Add the sausages, bacon, onion, and garlic and fry until the bacon and sausages are well browned.

Stir in the beans, tomatoes, tomato paste, maple syrup, brown sugar, mustard, salt, and pepper to taste (see below). Bring to a boil.

Sprinkle the bread crumbs over the surface and dot with the remaining butter or margarine.

Transfer the casserole to the oven and bake until most of the liquid has been absorbed by the beans and the top is crisp, about 1 hour.

ROAST RACK OF LAMB

—

THIS FESTIVE ROAST IS IDEAL FOR A DINNER PARTY. SERVE ON A HEAP OF COLORFUL
VEGETABLES FOR A DRAMATIC AND DELICIOUS EFFECT.

SERVES 4

*2 racks of lamb, each with 8 chops, ends of bones
    scraped clean*
¼ cup Dijon-style mustard
*1½ tablespoons fresh rosemary or 1 tablespoon
    dried rosemary*
salt and pepper
½ cup fine dry bread crumbs
¼ cup chopped fresh parsley
4 garlic cloves, minced
¼ cup olive oil
1 stick butter or margarine
1 cup chicken stock

Preheat the oven to 425°F.

Brush the meaty side of the racks with the mustard. Sprinkle with the rosemary, salt, and pepper.

In a bowl, mix the bread crumbs with the parsley, garlic, and half of the olive oil. Press this mixture evenly over the mustard on the racks of lamb (see below left). Wrap the scraped bone ends with foil. Put the racks in a roasting pan.

In a small saucepan, melt half the butter or margarine. Stir in the remaining olive oil. Drizzle this mixture over the crumb coating.

Roast the racks of lamb, allowing 40 minutes for medium-rare meat and 50 minutes for medium.

Transfer the racks to a warmed serving platter, arranging them so the bones are interlocked. Cover loosely with foil and set aside.

Pour the stock into the roasting pan and bring to a boil, scraping the bottom of the pan with a wooden spoon to mix in all the cooking juices. Remove from the heat and swirl in the remaining butter or margarine. Pour the gravy into a warmed sauceboat.

To serve, carve each rack by cutting down between the chop bones, or cut down after every 2 bones for double chops.

SOUTHERN FRIED CHICKEN

—

THIS BANNER DISH CAPTURES ALL THE WARMTH OF SOUTHERN HOSPITALITY IN ITS CRUNCHY
CRUST. A WELL-EXECUTED FRIED CHICKEN DISH WITH HUSH PUPPIES AND COLLARD GREENS ON
THE SIDE WILL MAKE SOUTHERN MEN DAB THEIR EYES AND BLESS THEIR GRANDMAS.

32

SERVES 4

½ cup buttermilk

1 3-pound chicken, cut into pieces

corn oil for frying

½ cup flour

1 tablespoon paprika

¼ teaspoon pepper

1 tablespoon water

Pour the buttermilk into a large bowl and add the chicken pieces. Stir to coat, then set aside for 5 minutes.

Heat a ¼-inch layer of oil in a large skillet over medium-high heat. Do not let oil overheat.

In a bowl or plastic bag, combine the flour, paprika, and pepper. One by one, lift the chicken pieces out of the buttermilk and dip into the flour to coat all over, shaking off any excess.

Add the chicken pieces to the hot oil and fry until lightly browned, about 10 minutes, turning over halfway through cooking time.

Reduce the heat to low and add the water to the skillet. Cover and cook 30 minutes, turning the pieces over at 10-minute intervals (see above). Uncover the pan and continue cooking until the chicken is very tender and the coating is crisp, about 15 minutes, turning every 5 minutes.

Serve hot with plenty of vegetables.

COOK'S TIP

YOUR LOCAL BUTCHER SHOULD CUT YOUR CHICKEN INTO PIECES. BUT IF DOING IT YOURSELF, ENSURE THAT THE LEGS ARE CUT INTO SMALLER PIECES THAN THE BREAST AS DARK MEAT COOKS MORE SLOWLY THAN LIGHT.

HONEY ROAST CHICKEN

A BRUSHING OF HONEY GIVES THIS BIRD AN IRRESISTIBLE CRISPY GOLDEN SKIN AND A SWEETNESS THAT COMPLEMENTS THE SMOKY BACON AND BREAD STUFFING.

SERVES 4

1 3½-pound chicken

2 tablespoons clear honey

1 tablespoon brandy

1½ tablespoons flour

⅔ cup chicken stock

FOR THE STUFFING

2 shallots, chopped

4 bacon slices, chopped

½ cup button mushrooms, quartered

1 tablespoon butter or margarine

2 thick slices of white bread, diced

1 tablespoon chopped fresh parsley

salt and pepper

For the stuffing, gently fry the shallots, bacon, and mushrooms in a skillet for about 5 minutes. With a slotted spoon, carefully transfer them all to a bowl.

Pour off all but 2 tablespoons of bacon fat from the pan. Add the butter or margarine to the pan and fry the bread until golden brown. Add the bread to the bacon mixture. Stir in the parsley and salt and pepper to taste. Let cool.

Preheat the oven to 350°F.

Pack the stuffing into the body cavity of the chicken. Truss it with string, or secure with poultry pins, to keep it in a neat shape.

Transfer the chicken to a roasting pan which just holds it comfortably.

Mix the honey with the brandy. Brush half of the mixture over the chicken. Roast until the chicken is thoroughly cooked, about 1 hour 20 minutes. To keep the chicken moist while cooking, baste the chicken frequently with the remaining honey mixture during roasting.

Transfer the chicken to a warmed serving platter. Cover with foil and set aside.

Pour all the cooking juices through a strainer into a degreasing pitcher. Set aside to let the fat rise to the surface.

Stir the flour into the sediments in the roasting pan. Add the lean part of the juices and the stock. Boil rapidly until the gravy has thickened, stirring constantly.

Pour the gravy into a warmed sauceboat and serve with the chicken.

34

CHICKEN POT PIE

—

THIS TRADITIONAL RECIPE IS WORTH EVERY MINUTE IT TAKES TO PREPARE. ONCE YOU HAVE
HAD HOMEMADE POT PIE YOU'LL NEVER SERVE STOREBOUGHT AGAIN.

36

SERVES 6

4 tablespoons butter or margarine

1 medium onion, chopped

3 carrots, cut into ½-inch dice

1 parsnip, cut into ½-inch dice

3 tablespoons flour

1½ cups chicken stock

⅓ cup medium sherry wine

⅓ cup dry white wine

¾ cup whipping cream

⅔ cup frozen peas, thawed and well
drained

3 cups cooked chicken meat, in
chunks

1 teaspoon dried thyme

1 tablespoon minced fresh parsley

salt and pepper

FOR THE CRUST

1⅓ cups flour

½ teaspoon salt

½ cup shortening

2-3 tablespoons ice water

1 egg

2 tablespoons milk

For the crust, sift the flour and salt into a mixing bowl. Using a pastry blender, cut in the shortening until the mixture resembles coarse crumbs. Sprinkle in the water, 1 tablespoon at a time, tossing lightly with a fork until the dough will form a ball. Remove the dough, dust with flour, wrap, and refrigerate until required.

Preheat the oven to 400°F.

Heat half of the butter or margarine in a medium saucepan. Add the onion, carrots, and parsnip and cook until softened, about 10 minutes. Remove the vegetables from the pan with a slotted spoon.

Melt the remaining butter or margarine in the saucepan. Add the flour and cook 5 minutes, stirring constantly. Stir in the stock, sherry, and white wine. Bring the sauce to a boil, and continue boiling for 1 minute, stirring constantly.

Add the cream, peas, chicken, thyme, and parsley to the sauce. Season to taste with salt and pepper. Simmer 1 minute, stirring.

Transfer the chicken mixture to a 2-quart shallow baking dish.

On a lightly floured surface, roll out the dough to ½-inch thickness. Lay the dough over the baking dish and trim off the excess. Dampen the rim of the

dish. With a fork, press the crust to the rim to seal.

Cut decorative shapes of stars and diamonds from the dough trimmings.

Lightly whisk the egg with the milk. Brush the pie crust all over with the egg wash. Arrange the dough shapes in an attractive design on top. Brush again with the egg wash. Make 1 or 2 holes in the crust so steam can escape during baking.

Bake the pie until the pastry is golden brown, about 35 minutes. Serve hot.

COUNTRY MEATLOAF

THERE ARE ALMOST AS MANY TYPES OF MEATLOAF AS THERE ARE COOKS IN AMERICA. EVERYONE HAS HIS OR HER OWN TWIST. THIS GOURMET VERSION CALLS FOR THREE KINDS OF GROUND MEAT, AND BACON SLICES LAID ACROSS THE TOP MAKE THE LOAF TENDER AND SUCCULENT.

SERVES 6

2 tablespoons butter or margarine

½ cup minced onion

2 garlic cloves, minced

½ cup minced celery

1 pound lean ground beef

½ pound ground veal

½ pound lean ground pork

2 eggs

1 cup fine fresh bread crumbs

½ cup chopped fresh parsley

2 tablespoons chopped fresh basil

½ teaspoon fresh or dried thyme leaves

½ teaspoon salt

½ teaspoon pepper

2 tablespoons Worcestershire sauce

¼ cup chili sauce or catsup

6 bacon slices

Preheat the oven to 350°F.

Melt the butter or margarine in a small skillet over low heat. Add the onion, garlic, and celery and cook until softened, 8-10 minutes. Remove from the heat and allow the mixture to cool slightly.

In a large mixing bowl combine the onion, garlic, and celery with all the other ingredients except the bacon. Mix together lightly, using a fork or your fingers. Do not overwork or the meat loaf will be too compact.

Form the meat mixture into an oval loaf. Carefully transfer it to a shallow baking pan.

Lay the bacon slices across the meatloaf (see above). Bake 1¼ hours, basting occasionally with the juices and bacon fat in the pan.

Remove from the oven and drain off the fat. Let the meat loaf stand for about 10 minutes before serving.

OLD-FASHIONED BEEF STEW

—

ON A COLD WINTER EVENING BEEF STEW IS THE PERFECT MEAL. IF YOU CAN, PREPARE IT
THE DAY BEFORE AND LET THE FLAVORS MELD. REHEAT AND SERVE WITH A FULL-BODIED RED
WINE OR HOT CIDER.

40

SERVES 6

3 tablespoons corn oil

1 large onion, sliced

2 carrots, chopped

1 celery stalk, chopped

2 tablespoons flour

3 tablespoons paprika

2 pounds beef chuck steak, cubed

2 tablespoons tomato paste

1 cup red wine

2 cups beef stock

1 sprig of fresh thyme or 1 teaspoon dried thyme

1 bay leaf

salt and pepper

3 medium potatoes, cut into 1½-inch pieces

1 cup button mushrooms, quartered

Preheat the oven to 375°F.

Heat half the oil in a large flameproof casserole. Add the onion, carrots, and celery and cook until softened, about 5 minutes. Remove the vegetables with a slotted spoon and set aside.

Combine the flour and paprika in a plastic bag. Add the beef cubes and shake to coat them with the seasoned flour (see right).

Heat the remaining oil in the casserole. Add the beef cubes and brown well on all sides for about 10 minutes.

Return the vegetables to the casserole. Stir in the tomato paste, red wine, stock, thyme, bay leaf, and a little salt and pepper. Bring to a boil.

Stir in the potatoes. Cover the casserole and transfer it to the oven. Cook 1 hour.

Stir in the mushrooms and continue cooking until the beef is very tender, about 30 minutes longer. Discard the bay leaf before serving.

CREAMY COLESLAW

A COOKOUT CLASSIC. NO BACKYARD BARBECUE
IS COMPLETE WITHOUT THIS TANGY SALAD.

SERVES 6

¾ pound green or white cabbage, cut in wedges
   and cored

¼ pound red cabbage, cored

3 scallions, finely chopped

2 medium carrots, grated

1 teaspoon sugar

2 tablespoons fresh lemon juice

2 teaspoons distilled white vinegar

½ cup sour cream

½ cup mayonnaise

¾ teaspoon celery seeds

salt and pepper

 Slice the green and red cabbage thinly across the leaves.

Place the cabbage in a mixing bowl and add the scallions and carrots. Toss to combine.

In a small bowl, combine the sugar, lemon juice, vinegar, sour cream, mayonnaise, and celery seeds.

Pour the mayonnaise dressing over the vegetables. Season with salt and pepper. Stir until well coated. Spoon into a serving bowl.

POTATO SALAD

SUBSTITUTE ANCHOVIES AND CAPERS FOR THE
TARRAGON FOR A PUNGENT ITALIAN VERSION.

SERVES 8

3 pounds small new potatoes

2 tablespoons white wine vinegar

1 tablespoon Dijon-style mustard

3 tablespoons vegetable or olive oil

½ cup chopped red onion

salt and pepper

½ cup mayonnaise

2 tablespoons chopped fresh tarragon or 1½
   teaspoons dried tarragon

½ cup thinly sliced celery

Cook the unpeeled potatoes in boiling salted water until tender, 15-20 minutes. Drain.

In a small bowl, mix together the vinegar and mustard until the mustard dissolves. Quickly whisk in the oil.

When the potatoes are cool enough to handle, slice them into a large mixing bowl.

Add the onion to the potatoes and pour the dressing over them. Season, then toss gently to combine. Let stand at least 30 minutes.

Mix together the mayonnaise and tarragon. Gently stir into the potatoes, along with the celery. Taste and adjust the seasoning before serving.

42

LONG-GRAIN AND WILD RICE RING

THIS AUTUMNAL RICE MOLD GOES ESPECIALLY WELL WITH ANY GAME DISH AS WELL AS
ROAST TURKEY OR CHICKEN.

44

SERVES 8

2 tablespoons corn oil

1 large onion, chopped

2 cups processed long-grain and wild rice

5 cups chicken stock

½ cup dried currants

salt

6 scallions, cut diagonally into ¼ inch pieces

parsley sprigs, for garnishing

Oil a 7-cup ring mold. Set aside.
Heat the oil in a large saucepan. Add the onion and cook until softened, about 5 minutes.

Add the rice to the pan and stir well to coat the rice with the oil.

Stir in the chicken stock and bring to a boil.

Reduce the heat to low. Stir the currants into the rice mixture. Add salt to taste. Cover and simmer until the rice is tender and all the stock has been absorbed by the rice, about 20 minutes.

Drain the rice if necessary and transfer it to a mixing bowl. Stir in the scallions.

Pack the rice mixture into the prepared mold (see above). Unmold it onto a warmed serving platter. If you like put parsley sprigs into the center of the ring before serving.

COOK'S TIP

TRUE WILD RICE IS CHEWY IN TEXTURE WITH A VERY EARTHY TASTE. PROCESSED VARIETIES HAVE LESS TASTE, BUT ARE USUALLY LESS EXPENSIVE. BE CAREFUL NOT TO OVERCOOK WILD RICE AS IT QUICKLY LOSES ITS FRAGRANCE AND ROBUST TEXTURE.

CREAMED CORN WITH BELL PEPPERS

—

PREPARE THIS DISH IN LATE SUMMER WHEN
CORN AND PEPPERS ARE AT THEIR PEAK.

46

SERVES 4

2 tablespoons butter or margarine
1 small red bell pepper, seeded and finely diced
1 small green bell pepper, seeded and finely diced
4 ears of corn, husks and silk removed
½ cup whipping cream
salt and pepper

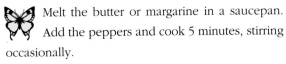 Melt the butter or margarine in a saucepan. Add the peppers and cook 5 minutes, stirring occasionally.

Cut the kernels off the ears of corn. Scrape the cobs with the back of a knife to extract the milky liquid. Alternatively, use a corn scraper to remove the kernels and liquid.

Add the corn kernels with the liquid to the saucepan. Stir in the cream. Bring to a boil and simmer until thickened and the corn is tender, about 3-4 minutes. Season with salt and pepper and serve as an accompaniment side dish.

VARIATION

2 CUPS FROZEN WHOLE-KERNEL CORN, THAWED, CAN BE
SUBSTITUTED IF FRESH CORN IS NOT AVAILABLE.

FRIED OKRA AND CORNMEAL

—

THIS DISH IS CONSIDERED AN ACQUIRED TASTE
BUT WHEN FRIED THE MORSELS ARE ADDICTIVE.

SERVES 6

1½ pounds okra
½ cup yellow cornmeal
⅛ teaspoon black pepper
⅓ cup bacon drippings
  or corn oil
¾ teaspoon salt

 Wash the okra well and drain in a colander. Cut off the stems.

Combine the cornmeal and pepper in a mixing bowl. Add the still damp okra and toss to coat evenly with cornmeal.

Heat the bacon drippings or oil in a skillet. Add the okra and fry until tender and golden, about 4-5 minutes. Drain on paper towels.

Sprinkle the fried okra with the salt just before serving and toss lightly.

COOK'S TIP

WHEN REMOVING THE STEMS OF THE OKRA, SLICE
THROUGH THE POINT WHERE IT JOINS THE VEGETABLE.
CUTTING INTO THE VEGETABLE ALLOWS THE RELEASE OF
THE VISCOUS INSIDES.

CHEESY BREAD PUDDING

—

THIS HOMEY SIDE DISH CAN STAND ON ITS OWN AS A WINTER LUNCH WITH A CUP OF SOUP OR GRACE A SIDEBOARD AT A FORMAL DINNER PARTY.

48

SERVES 4

3 tablespoons butter or margarine, at room
temperature

2½ cups milk

3 eggs, beaten

½ cup freshly grated Parmesan cheese

⅛ teaspoon cayenne

salt and pepper

5 large, thick slices of crusty white bread

2 cups shredded cheddar cheese

 Grease an oval baking dish with the butter or margarine.

In a bowl combine the milk, eggs, 3 tablespoons of the Parmesan cheese, the cayenne, and salt and pepper to taste.

Cut the bread slices in half. Arrange 5 of them in the bottom of the prepared dish, overlapping the slices if necessary.

Sprinkle the bread with two-thirds of the cheddar cheese. Top with the remaining bread.

Pour the egg mixture evenly over the bread. Press the bread down gently so that it will absorb the egg mixture. Sprinkle the top evenly with the remaining Parmesan and cheddar cheeses (see left). Let stand until most of the egg mixture has been absorbed, at least 30 minutes.

Preheat the oven to 425°F.

Set the baking dish in a roasting pan. Add enough boiling water to the pan to come halfway up the sides of the baking dish.

Place in the oven and bake 30 minutes, or until the pudding is lightly set and browned. If the pudding browns too quickly, before setting, cover loosely with foil. Serve hot.

BABY BAKED POTATOES WITH BLUE CHEESE TOPPING

—

USE THE SMALLEST POTATOES YOU CAN FIND — THEY SHOULD REALLY BE BITE-SIZED. IF YOU CAN, COOK THEM OUTDOORS, THE COMBINATION OF SMOKY POTATO SKIN AND CREAMY TOPPING IS DELICIOUS.

50

MAKES 20

20 small new potatoes
¼ cup vegetable oil
coarse salt
½ cup sour cream
¼ cup crumbled blue cheese
2 tablespoons chopped fresh chives

Preheat the oven to 350°F.

Wash and dry the potatoes. Pour the oil into a bowl. Add the potatoes and toss for a few seconds to coat well with oil.

Dip the potatoes in the coarse salt to coat lightly. Spread out the potatoes on a baking sheet. Bake until tender, 45-50 minutes.

In a small bowl, combine the sour cream and blue cheese together.

Cut a cross in the top of each potato (see above). Press with your fingers to open the potatoes.

Top each potato with a dollop of the cheese mixture. Sprinkle with chives and serve immediately as a delicious accompaniment or light snack.

PUMPKIN PIE

—

THANKSGIVING MEALS ALMOST ALWAYS END WITH THIS HARVEST PIE. TRY TO GET A FRESH PUMPKIN AND MAKE YOUR OWN PURÉE — IT TASTES WONDERFUL, THOUGH CANNED IS A PERFECTLY ACCEPTABLE SUBSTITUTE. A TABLESPOON OF RUM ADDS A PIRATICAL FLAVOR TO THE FILLING.

SERVES 8

1½ cups pumpkin purée

2 cups light cream

⅔ cup light brown sugar, firmly packed

¼ teaspoon salt

1 teaspoon ground cinnamon

½ teaspoon ground ginger

¼ teaspoon ground cloves

⅛ teaspoon grated nutmeg

2 eggs

FOR THE CRUST

1⅓ cups flour

½ teaspoon salt

½ cup shortening

2-3 tablespoons ice water

¼ cup pecans, chopped

Preheat the oven to 425°F.

For the crust, sift the flour and salt into a mixing bowl. Using a pastry blender, cut in the shortening until the mixture resembles coarse crumbs. Sprinkle in the water, 1 tablespoon at a time, tossing lightly until the dough will form a ball.

On a lightly-floured surface, roll out the dough to ¼-inch thickness. Use it to line a 9-inch pie pan, easing the dough in and being careful not to stretch it. Trim off the excess dough.

If you like, use the dough trimmings to make a decorative rope edge. Cut in strips and twist together in pairs. Dampen the rim of the pie shell and press on the rope edge. Sprinkle the chopped pecans over the bottom of the pie shell (see above).

With a whisk or an electric mixer on medium speed, beat together the pumpkin purée, cream, brown sugar, salt, spices, and eggs.

Pour the pumpkin mixture into the pie shell. Bake 10 minutes, then reduce the heat to 350°F and continue baking until the filling is set, about 45 minutes. Let the pie cool in the pan, set on a wire rack.

HAZELNUT BROWNIES

—

THESE DENSE AND FUDGY CHOCOLATE SQUARES ARE ALWAYS A BIG HIT. SERVE WITH TALL
GLASSES OF COLD MILK AND WATCH THEM DISAPPEAR.

MAKES 9

2 1-ounce squares unsweetened chocolate

5 tablespoons butter or margarine

1 cup sugar

7 tablespoons flour

½ teaspoon baking powder

2 eggs, beaten

½ teaspoon vanilla extract

1 cup skinned hazelnuts, roughly chopped

 Preheat the oven to 350°F. Grease an 8-inch square baking pan.

In a heatproof bowl set over a pan of barely simmering water, or in a double boiler, melt the chocolate and butter or margarine. Remove from the heat.

Add the sugar, flour, baking powder, eggs, vanilla, and ½ cup of the hazelnuts to the melted mixture and stir.

Pour the batter into the prepared pan.

Bake 10 minutes, then sprinkle the reserved hazelnuts on the top. Return to the oven and bake until firm to the touch, 25 minutes.

Let cool in the pan, set on a wire rack for 10 minutes, then unmold onto the rack and let cool completely. Cut into squares for serving (see above).

APPLE PIE

—

EVERY ONCE IN A WHILE THE WEARY SOUL NEEDS A BIG WEDGE OF HOMEMADE APPLE PIE.
THIS RECIPE FITS THE BILL. SERVING THE PIE A LA MODE (WITH ICE CREAM) IS EVEN MORE
RESTORATIVE.

SERVES 8

6 cups peeled and sliced tart apples, such as
Granny Smith (about 2 pounds)

1 tablespoon fresh lemon juice

1 teaspoon vanilla extract

½ cup sugar

½ teaspoon ground cinnamon

1½ tablespoons butter or
margarine

1 egg yolk

2 teaspoons whipping cream

FOR THE CRUST

2 cups flour

1 teaspoon salt

¾ cup shortening

4-5 tablespoons ice water

1 tablespoon quick-cooking tapioca

Preheat the oven to 450°F.

For the crust, sift the flour and salt into a mixing bowl. Using a pastry blender, cut in the shortening until the mixture resembles coarse crumbs.

Sprinkle in the water, 1 tablespoon at a time, tossing lightly with your fingertips or with a fork until the dough will form a ball, about 10 minutes.

Divide the dough in half and shape each half into a ball. On a lightly-floured surface, roll out one of the balls to a circle about 12 inches in diameter.

Use it to line a 9-inch pie pan, easing the dough in and being careful not to stretch it. Trim off the excess dough and use the trimmings for decorating. Sprinkle the tapioca evenly over the bottom of the pie shell.

Roll out the remaining dough to ⅛-inch thickness. With a sharp knife, cut out 8 large leaf-shapes. Cut the trimmings into small leaf shapes. Score the leaves with the back of the knife to mark veins.

In a bowl, toss together the apples with the lemon juice, vanilla, sugar, and cinnamon. Fill the pie shell with the apple mixture and dot with the butter or margarine.

Arrange the large pastry leaves in a decorative pattern on top. Decorate the edge with small leaves.

Mix together the egg yolk and cream and brush over the leaves to glaze them.

Bake 10 minutes, then reduce the heat to 350°F and continue baking until the pastry is golden brown, 35-45 minutes. Let the pie cool in the pan, set on a wire rack.

APPLE AND PEAR SKILLET CAKE

—

A TASTY DESSERT THAT TAKES FULL ADVANTAGE OF LATE SUMMER'S FRUIT HARVEST.

58

SERVES 6

1 apple, peeled, cored, and thinly sliced

1 pear, peeled, cored, and thinly sliced

½ cup walnut pieces, chopped

1 teaspoon ground cinnamon

1 teaspoon grated nutmeg

3 eggs

¼ cup flour

2 tablespoons light brown sugar, firmly packed

¾ cup milk

1 teaspoon vanilla extract

4 tablespoons butter or margarine

confectioners' sugar, for sprinkling

Preheat the oven to 375°F. In a mixing bowl, toss together the apple slices, pear slices, walnuts, cinnamon and nutmeg. Set aside.

With an electric mixer, beat together the eggs, flour, brown sugar, milk, and vanilla.

Melt the butter or margarine in a 9- or 10-inch ovenproof skillet (preferably castiron) over medium heat. Add the apple mixture. Cook until lightly caramelized, about 5 minutes, stirring occasionally (see left).

Pour the batter over the fruit and nuts. Transfer the skillet to the oven and bake until the cake is puffy and pulling away from the sides of the pan, about 30 minutes.

Sprinkle the cake lightly with confectioners' sugar and serve hot.

COOK'S TIP

THIS SIMPLE CAKE CAN BE MADE WITH A VARIETY OF FRUITS: TRY A MACINTOSH APPLE AND A BARTLETT PEAR, OR A GRANNY SMITH APPLE AND A COMICE PEAR. THIS DISH ALSO MAKES A GOOD BREAKFAST PASTRY.

DEVIL'S FOOD CAKE

—

WHEN CAKE FANCIERS PICTURE THE PERFECT CHOCOLATE CAKE, THIS LIGHT-TEXTURED, RICHLY FROSTED VERSION MOST OFTEN COMES TO MIND. IF SOMEONE YOU LOVE REQUESTS A CHOCOLATE BIRTHDAY CAKE, THIS IS THE ONE TO MAKE.

SERVES 10

4 1-ounce squares semisweet chocolate

1½ cups milk

1 cup light brown sugar, firmly packed

1 egg yolk

2¼ cups cake flour

1 teaspoon baking soda

½ teaspoon salt

1 cup (2 sticks) butter or margarine, at room temperature

2 cups granulated sugar

4 eggs

1 teaspoon vanilla extract

FOR THE FROSTING

8 1-ounce squares semisweet chocolate

¾ cup sour cream

¼ teaspoon salt

 Preheat the oven to 350°F. Line 2 8- or 9-inch round cake pans with wax paper.

In a heatproof bowl set over a pan of simmering water, or in a double boiler, combine the chocolate, ½ cup of the milk, the brown sugar, and egg yolk. Cook, stirring, until smooth and thickened. Let cool.

Sift the flour, baking soda, and salt into a small bowl. Set aside.

With an electric mixer, cream the butter or margarine with the granulated sugar until light and fluffy. Beat in the whole eggs, one at a time. Mix in the vanilla.

On low speed, beat the flour mixture into the butter mixture alternately with the remaining milk, beginning and ending with flour.

Pour in the mixture and mix until just combined.

Divide the batter evenly between the cake pans. Bake until a cake tester inserted in the center comes out clean, 25-30 minutes.

Let cool in the pans on wire racks for 10 minutes, then unmold the cakes from the pans onto the wire racks and let cool completely.

For the frosting, melt the chocolate in a heat-proof bowl set over a pan of hot, not boiling, water, or in the top of a double boiler. Remove from the heat and stir in sour cream and salt. Let cool.

Set 1 cake layer on a serving plate and spread with one-third of the frosting. Place the second cake layer on top. Spread the remaining frosting all over the top and sides of the cake, swirling it to make a decorative finish.

APPLE MAPLE DUMPLINGS

—

100% PURE VERMONT MAPLE SYRUP IS AN ESSENTIAL INGREDIENT IN THESE TASTY DUMPLINGS. COMMERCIAL BRANDS ARE WATERED DOWN AND DON'T HAVE THE INTENSE MAPLE TASTE.

62

SERVES 8

4½ cups flour

2 teaspoons salt

1½ cups shortening

¾-1 cup ice water

8 firm, tart-sweet apples

1 egg white

⅔ cup sugar

3 tablespoons whipping cream

½ teaspoon vanilla extract

1 cup maple syrup

whipped cream, for serving

Sift the flour and salt into a large bowl. Using a pastry blender or 2 knives, cut in the shortening until the mixture resembles coarse meal. Sprinkle with ¾ cup water and mix until the dough holds together. If it is too crumbly, add a little more water. Gather into a ball. Wrap in wax paper and refrigerate at least 20 minutes.

Preheat the oven to 425°F.

Peel the apples. Remove the cores, cutting from the stem end, without cutting through the base.

Roll out the dough thinly. Cut squares almost large enough to enclose the apples. Brush the squares with egg white. Set an apple in the center of each square of dough.

Combine the sugar, cream, and vanilla in a small bowl. Spoon some into the hollow in each apple.

Pull the points of the dough squares up around the apples and moisten the edges where they overlap. Mold the dough around the apples, pleating the top. Take care not to cover the center hollows. Crimp the edges tightly together to seal.

Set the apples in a large greased baking dish, at least ¾ inch apart. Bake for 30 minutes. Lower the oven temperature to 350°F and continue baking until the pastry turns golden brown and the apples become tender, approximately 20 minutes more.

Transfer the dumplings to a serving dish. Mix the maple syrup with the juices in a baking dish and drizzle over the dumplings.

Serve the dumplings hot with plenty of whipped cream.

INDEX

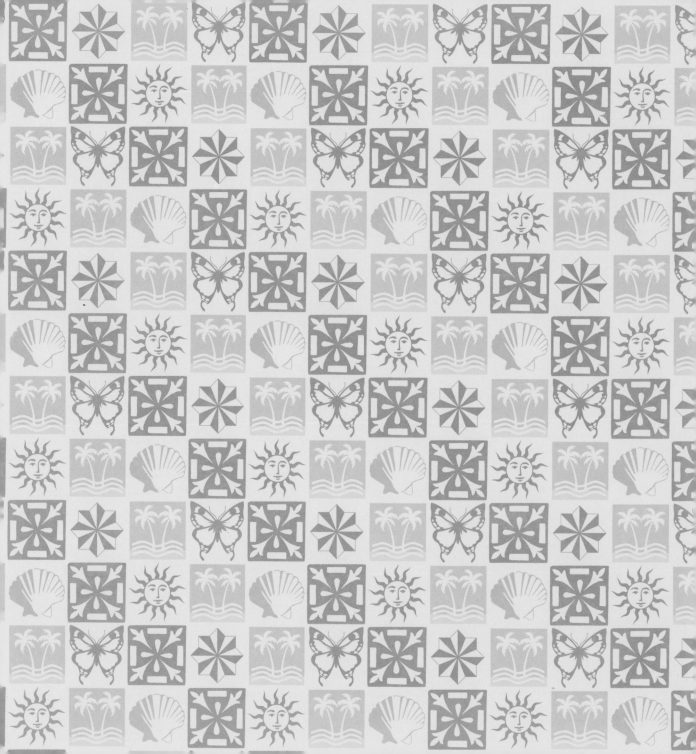